Paper Tags and Cards

•FLORENCE TEMKO•

The Millbrook Press
Brookfield, Connecticut

Published in the United States
in 1997 by

The Millbrook Press, Inc.
2 Old New Milford Road
Brookfield, Connecticut 06804

First published in Great Britain in 1995 by

Dragon's World Limited
London House, Great Eastern Wharf
Parkgate Road, LONDON SW11 4NQ

© 1995 Dragon's World
Text and paper project designs
© 1995 Florence Temko

Text: Florence Temko
Editor: Kyla Barber
Design: Mel Raymond, Bob Scott
Illustrations: John Walls
Art Director: John Strange
Editorial Director: Pippa Rubinstein

Library of Congress Cataloging-in-Publication Data
Temko, Florence.
  Paper tags and cards / Florence Temko.
    p. cm. -- (Paper magic)
  British ed. published in 1995 under the title: Cards and tags.
  Summary: Provides step-by-step instructions for making a variety of
greeting cards and gift tags, as well as a section with directions for making
your own paper.
  ISBN 0-7613-0210-7 (lib. ed.).
  1. Greeting cards--Juvenile literature. 2. Invitation cards--Juvenile
literature. 3. Paper work--Juvenile literature. 4. Papermaking--Juvenile
literature. [1. Greeting cards. 2. Paper work. 3. Handicraft.]
I. Title. II. Series: Temko, Florence. Paper magic.
TT872.T46 1997
745.594'1--dc20
                                    96-28133
                                    CIP
                                    AC

Printed in Italy

CONTENTS

One, two, or three stars next to a heading indicate the degree of difficulty.

Easy

⭐

You can do it

⭐⭐

For experts!

⭐⭐⭐

Making your own greeting cards is fun and can save you money, too. You can start off with a basic design and add on glitter, confetti, leaves, and other decorations. Every card is unique.

The designs in this book are arranged in the same way. A basic design is followed with suggestions for how you can make it more exciting. The color and texture of the paper you choose often makes the difference between a so-so card and a really special one.

Most of the cards take only minutes to make, but I have included a few that take longer. They're worth the effort because they may hide a surprise.

They're fun for you to make and even more fun for the friends who will receive them.

When you make your own cards you can help the environment by using recycled paper. Many stationery and office supply stores sell recycled paper and cardboard in soft colors and interesting textures.

You can reuse and recycle in other ways. When you make cards you often cut off small pieces of paper. They are colorful and may have interesting shapes. Use them to decorate your cards, along with natural materials like leaves, twigs, and even dried herbs that are sitting on the kitchen shelf.

KEY

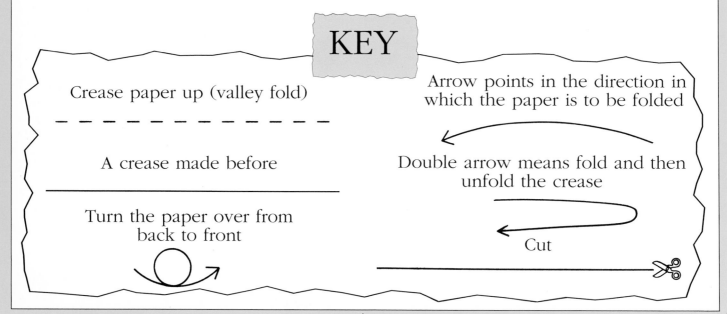

Crease paper up (valley fold)

A crease made before

Turn the paper over from back to front

Arrow points in the direction in which the paper is to be folded

Double arrow means fold and then unfold the crease

Cut

ABOUT PAPER AND SUPPLIES

Almost any kind of paper can be turned into greeting cards and invitations. At the beginning of each project you will find a listing of the paper and other materials you need.

Paper: Stationery, computer paper, printing paper, giftwrap, or colored art paper.

Stiff paper or thin cardboard: This is about the same stiffness and weight that you find in ready-made greeting cards. Choose cardboard, or card, construction paper, poster paper or posterboard, Bristol paper, index cards, or oaktag. Sharpen any creases by going over them with a ruler.

Reuse, recycle

Before you throw away any piece of paper, think about whether you could use it for making a card. As you make the things shown in this book, you will be cutting up a lot of paper. You can easily recycle all those funny shapes that fall off. Turn them into stickers that you glue on other cards.

Glue

You can use your favorite glue, but always spread on as little as possible. Otherwise, the paper may buckle. My favorite glues are white glue and glue sticks (they must be fresh).

With certain types of glue sticks the paper may be lifted off again so that you can rearrange a design until you're satisfied with it.

Measurements

All dimensions are given in centimeters and inches. They are not always exactly equal to avoid too many fractions. Either set will work well.

Anything goes

In this book I have tried to show how to make cards in many different ways. You can create many other cards by mixing the design for one card with the decorations suggested for another card. Have fun adding all kinds of confetti, ribbons, paper cutouts, seeds, snipped-up pieces of colorful paper, even feathers. Anything goes!

HOW TO MAKE ENVELOPES

Usually you can use normal envelopes for the cards you make, but sometimes you may need an envelope for an odd size, for an extra-large card or to match the color of the card inside. You can make envelopes in any size from plain paper or patterned giftwrap. If the paper is dark or has a busy pattern, write the receiver's address on a white label.

You will need
Plain paper, giftwrap, or thin card
Scissors, glue

1 Place the card in the middle of the envelope paper. Fold the paper around all four edges of the card. Leave very narrow spaces on all sides to allow the card to slide in and out easily.

2 Open the paper flat and cut away the four corners, A, B, C, D shown in the drawing.

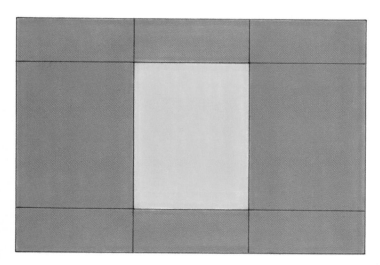

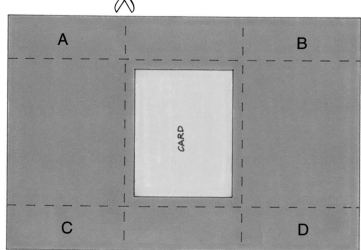

3 Fold in the sides. Fold up the bottom of the paper and glue it to the sides. Fold down the top flap. Make some interesting paper shapes in different colored paper and use one to fasten each envelope.

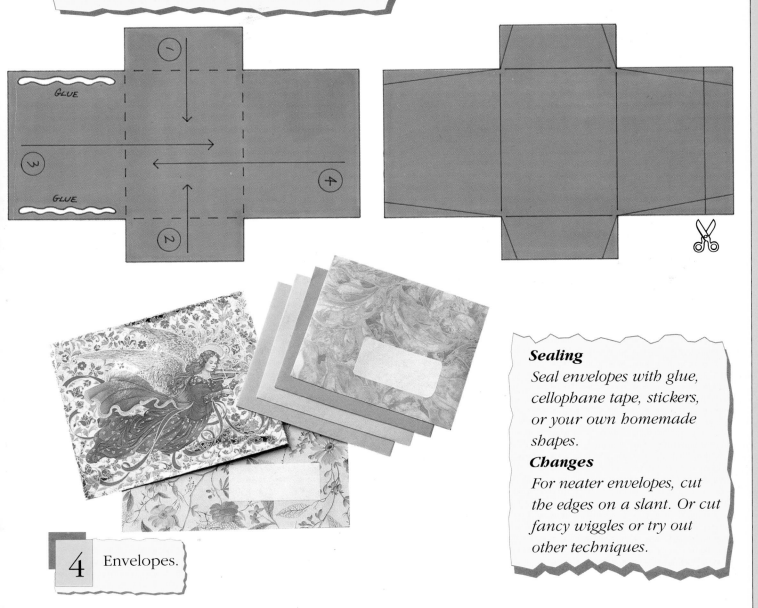

4 Envelopes.

Sealing

Seal envelopes with glue, cellophane tape, stickers, or your own homemade shapes.

Changes

For neater envelopes, cut the edges on a slant. Or cut fancy wiggles or try out other techniques.

HOW TO MAKE INSERTS

You may have seen cards with extra pieces of paper inside. They are called inserts.

You will need
A card
A piece of white paper
Scissors, glue

1 Cut a piece of white paper a little smaller than the card. Fold it in half.

2 Apply a narrow strip of glue next to the crease of the insert.

3 Open the card and glue the insert inside.

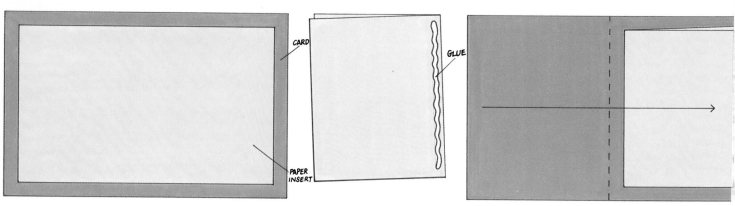

CARD

PAPER INSERT

GLUE

4 Card with insert.

Inserts with ribbons

You can hold a card and insert together with a ribbon. Let the ends hang down below the knot at the bottom of the card.

HAVE A HEART

For Valentine's Day or any other occasion, fold a piece of paper into a heart. Send it off just that way or glue it to a blank card.

You will need
A piece of red paper 5 by 10 inches (15 by 30 cm), or any piece of paper in the proportion of 1 to 2

★ ★

1 Fold the paper in half. Unfold the paper flat.

2 Fold the sides to the middle.

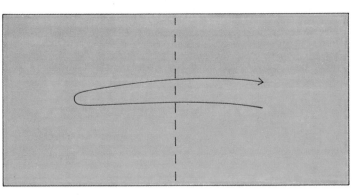

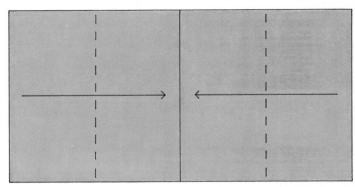

3 Turn the paper over from front to back.

4 At the bottom, fold the corners neatly to the middle crease. At the top, fold the outside corners in just a little.

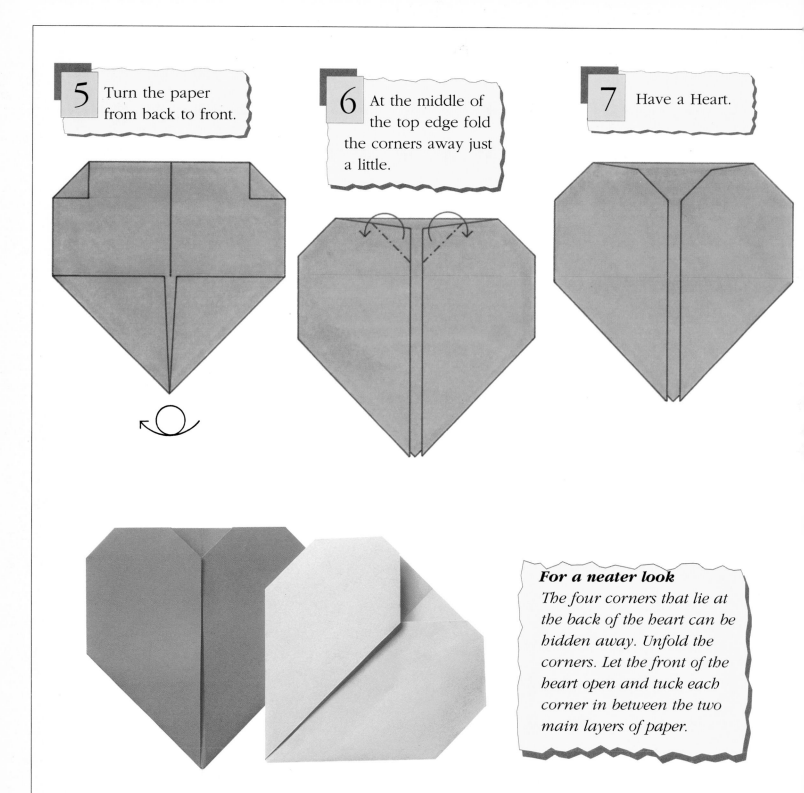

5 Turn the paper from back to front.

6 At the middle of the top edge fold the corners away just a little.

7 Have a Heart.

For a neater look

The four corners that lie at the back of the heart can be hidden away. Unfold the corners. Let the front of the heart open and tuck each corner in between the two main layers of paper.

SHELL POP-UP

Pop-up cards are special, and this one is very easy to construct. All you need to do is shape the top of the card with a curve and a shell will pop up when the card is opened.

1 Cut the piece of paper in half.

2 Fold both pieces in half like this.

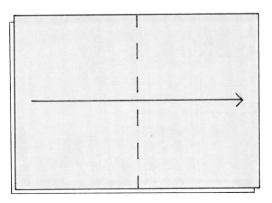

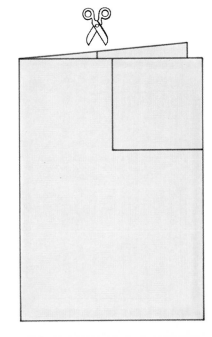

3 On one piece cut away a 2-inch (5-centimeter) square at the open edge.

4 Draw a curve, as shown. Cut on the line.

5 Bend down the curve.

6 Cut a very narrow sliver off the side edges. Open the paper.

PUSH

7 Draw on a shell. Close the paper, pushing the shell inside. The shell is hidden in between the two main layers of paper. Sharpen the creases.

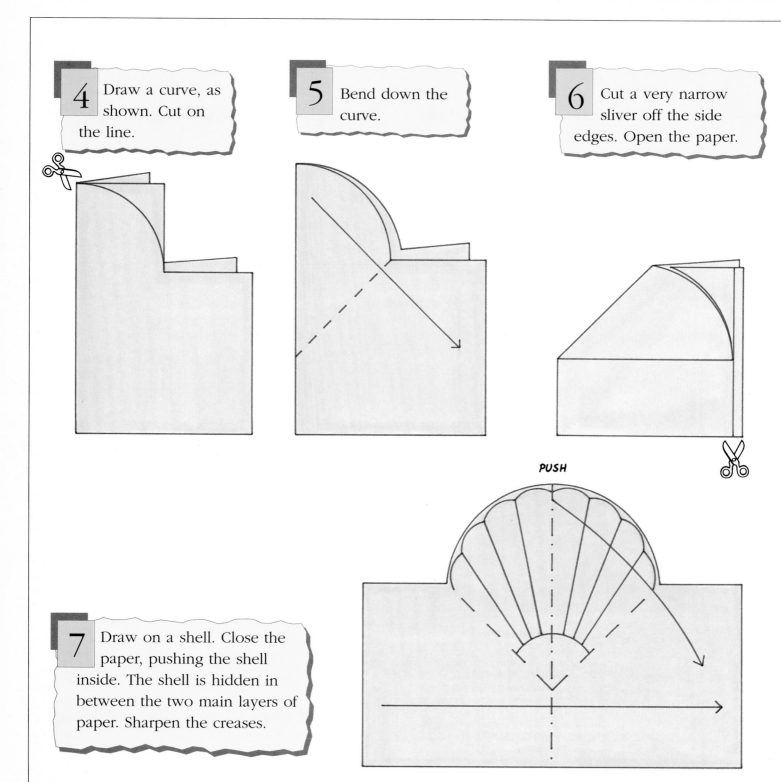

8 Glue the shell pop-up inside the second piece of paper.

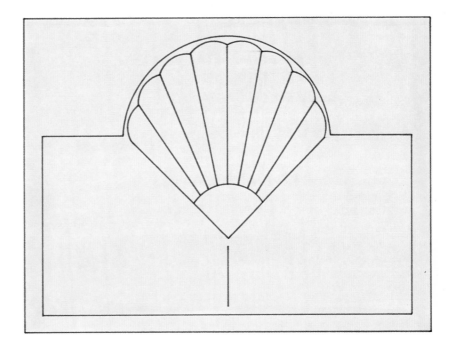

9 Shell Pop-Up.

Decorations

Decorate the front of the card with shells, waves, and with anything else you like. You could glue on sand: Spread a thin layer of glue. Sprinkle on sand. Let the glue dry. Pour off any loose sand.

HALLOWEEN INVITATIONS

Make these cards for invitations to Halloween or fancy-dress parties.

You will need
Stiff black paper
Colored paper scraps
White paper
Scissors, pencil, glue

1 **For the Black Cat**
Cut paper 4 by 12 inches (10 by 30 centimeters). Make a pencil mark on the middle of the long edge. Fold both narrow edges to the pencil mark.

2 Cut the sides into curves.

3 Cut ears at the top. Note that the tops of the ears are flat, leaving some of the folded edge. If you cut the ears into sharp points the paper will fall apart.

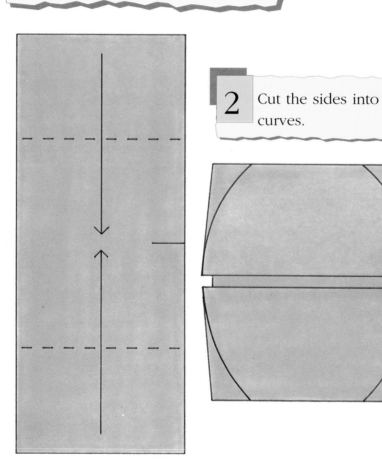

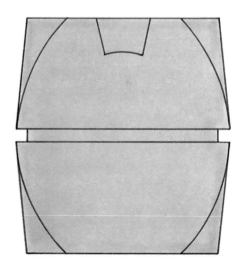

4 Cut paper scraps for eyes, whiskers, and feet. Cut a piece of white paper. Glue it inside for writing your invitation or other message.

Scary Bat

1 Cut a piece of paper the same size as for the cat and fold in half.

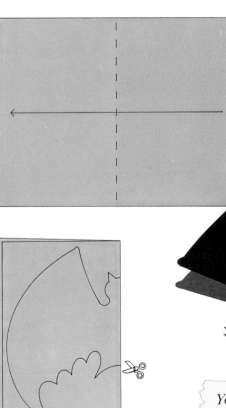

2 Trace the outline of half a bat and put the tracing paper over the black card, with its body at the fold line. Cut through both pieces of paper.

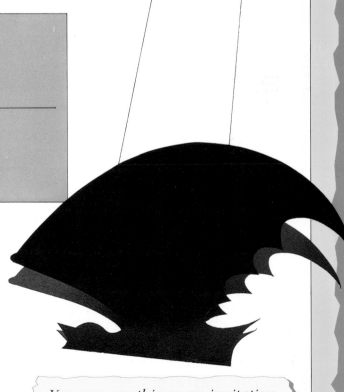

You can use this as an invitation, or hang it as a mobile.

3-D BUTTERFLY

Open the card and a butterfly or a rocket pops up. It's your choice. Of course, you could put a mouse there or anything else. It's the same surprise.

You will need
*A piece of stiff paper or thin card,
8½ by 11 inches (21 by 28 cm)
Colored paper
Scissors, glue, felt-tip pens*

1 Cut the piece of paper in half.

FOR THE CARD

FOR THE STRIP

2 One piece is for the card. Fold it in half.

3 From the other piece cut a strip 1½ inches (4 cm) wide, as shown. Cut 1 inch (2 cm) off the end of the strip.

4 Fold the strip in half. Unfold it. Fold the edges to the crease.

16

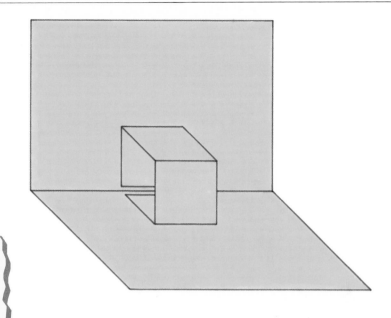

5 Put dabs of glue on the end panels and glue them to the inside of the card.

6 Cut out a butterfly. Color it any way you like. Glue it to the front of the pop-up. When you close the card the butterfly must be completely hidden inside.

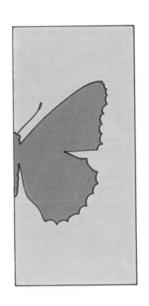

7 3-D Butterfly.

Write the message

Decorate the front and inside of the pop-up with small cut-outs, stickers, or rubber stampings, but leave room to write your message.

KIMONO CARD

The kimono on this card is folded according to the ancient rules of origami without any cutting or gluing. Many people who like puzzles enjoy origami. You can solve the kimono puzzle by following both the text and drawings slowly and carefully. Choose giftwrap with an Oriental design or patterned origami paper.

You will need
*A piece of giftwrap,
12 by 4 inches
(30 by 10 centimeters)
Pencil, ruler,
blank card*

1 Begin with the white side of the paper up. Fold the top edge over about 3/8 inch (.75 centimeter).

2 TURN THE PAPER OVER.

3 Mark the middle of the top edge with pencil or by creasing a small nick. Fold both corners to the middle, beginning the creases at the mark.

4 Make a valley fold 4 inches (10 cm) up from the bottom edge.

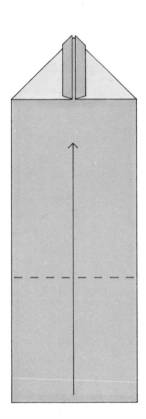

5 Mountain fold to the BACK as shown.

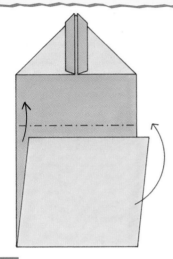

6 Bring both side edges to lie against the collar, but leave the bottom layer alone. To permit the paper to lie flat you must spread the top into a triangle.

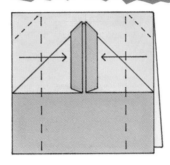

7 Mountain fold the top edge to the BACK, but leave the pointed collar alone.

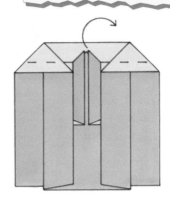

8 Mountain fold the bottom layer of the paper to the BACK to show the sleeves. Glue the kimono to the front of a blank card.

9 Kimono Card.

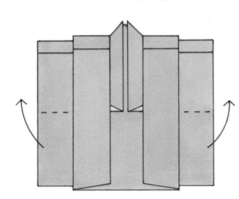

Other sizes

You can make bigger or smaller kimonos when you use bigger or smaller pieces of paper. Always cut the paper three times as long as it is wide.

Add decorations

Decorate your card with glitter, rubber stampings, or colored markers.

HIDDEN MESSAGE

A magician sometimes performs this trick at the end of a show because it's such a great act. It looks as if he or she is cutting an ordinary snowflake from a folded piece of paper. But when the paper is unfolded it spells a message. It may say "Happy Birthday," the name of the school where the performance is taking place, or something else. Everybody is surprised when the paper is opened. Always practice the trick on your own before performing it in front of others.

You will need
A full-size sheet of newspaper
Scissors, wide marker

1 Cut the paper into a 20-inch (50-cm) square. Fold the paper in quarters.

2 In the picture, M is the corner which is the middle of the paper. Fold corner A to corner B.

A

M   B

3 Fold it in half.

M

4 Make two creases 1¹/₂ inches (4 cm) apart, exactly where shown. Unfold the paper flat.

HIDDEN MESSAGE

M

5 Write HAPPY BIRTHDAY (or any other words) between the creased lines in bold capital letters. Then cut out the letters carefully.

6 Refold the paper. Now practice the trick until it's perfect!

7 Hidden Message.

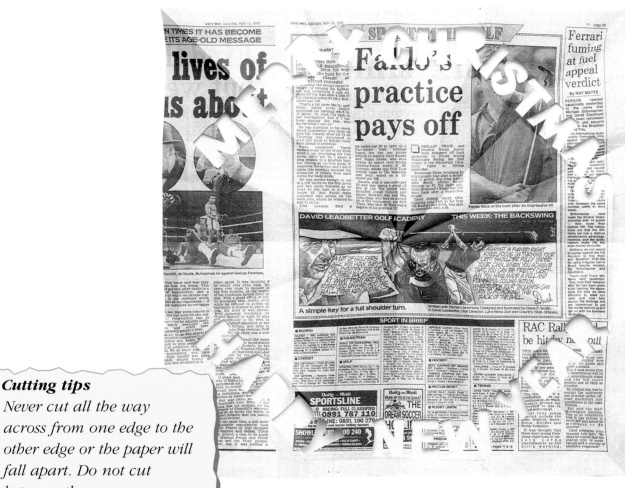

Cutting tips
Never cut all the way across from one edge to the other edge or the paper will fall apart. Do not cut between the creases or you will ruin the message.

VALENTINE WOVEN HEART

This heart is very special—you can fill it with little presents. You could even hang it as a decoration.

★★

You will need
*Red and white paper
Scissors, glue*

1 From each sheet of paper cut a piece 4 by 12 inches (10 by 30 centimeters). Fold each piece of paper in half the short way.

2 Beginning at the folded edge, cut 1-inch (2.5-cm) strips, ending about 1 inch (2.5 cm) away from the opposite end.

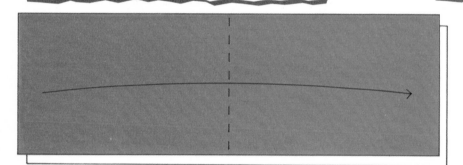

3 Place strip A between the layers of strip 1. Place strip 2 between the layers of strip A. Continue weaving by repeating these two steps.

4 Push strip A up and then weave strip B by first placing strip 1 between the layers of strip B. Then place strip B between the layers of strip 2 and so on.

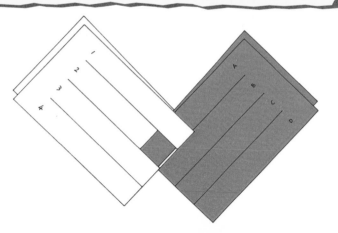

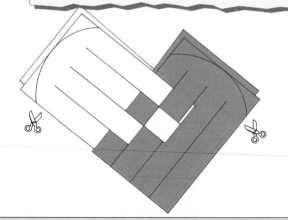

5 Weave strip C as you did strip A and weave strip D as you did strip B. Cut the top edges to make them rounded.

6 Cut two strips of paper 2 by 12 inches (5 by 30 centimeters). Make a handle using both strips as shown.

7 Glue the handle to the inside of the heart.

8 Woven Heart.

FANCY TOPS

Make a card with a difference. Instead of just drawing a picture on a card, you can make the picture part of the card!

You will need
*Stiff colored paper
Scissors, felt-tip pens
Glue, glitter,
giftwrap for
decoration*

1 Fold the piece of colored paper in half lengthwise.

2 Draw a house roof shape and chimney at the top of the card. Cut around the roof and chimney.

3 Draw on windows, a door, roof tiles, and anything else you can think of. Use scraps of giftwrap as decoration. Add snow to the roof for a Christmas card.

A house card makes a good "housewarming" card, but you can make all sorts of shapes. A car-shaped card for good luck for a driving test, a Christmas tree-shaped card, a butterfly-shaped card... anything goes!

FOLDED CHRISTMAS CARD

This is a very special Christmas card, made using a cutting and folding method.

You will need
*Stiff colored paper or card 5 by 7 inches (13 by 18 cm)
Patterned giftwrap
Ruler, pencil,
Scissors, glue*

1 Cut a piece of paper 3 by $4^3/_4$ inches (8 by 12 centimeters) and fold the paper in half.

2 Draw a pencil line from corner to corner. Cut on the line through both layers of paper.

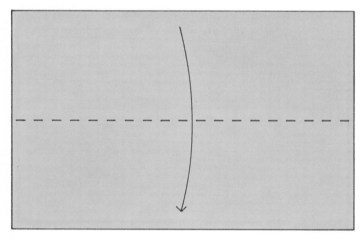

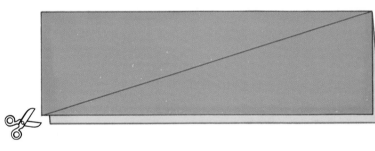

3 Cut parallel slits at an angle, beginning and ending about $1/_4$ inch (.5 centimeter) away from the edges. Unfold the paper.

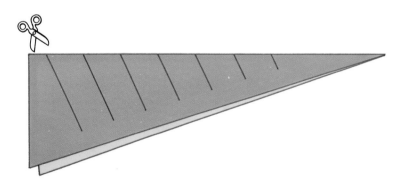

4 Fold up all the triangles, as shown.

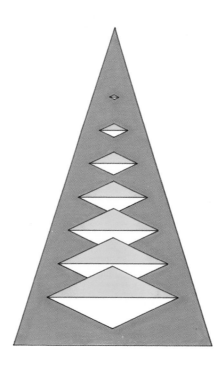

5 Glue one, two, or three trees on the card. Stick a gold star at the top of each, or draw one on.

SECRET CARD

Send a secret message to someone in a card sealed with ribbon.

You will need
Colored card
Giftwrap, felt-tip pens, glue
Scissors, pencil, colored ribbon

1 Fold the card in half and open it out again.

2 With a pencil, draw two lines about 1 inch (2 cm) long in the middle of the outside edges of your card.

3 Use the point of a small pair of scissors to make a hole in the paper somewhere on the line, and cut along the line.

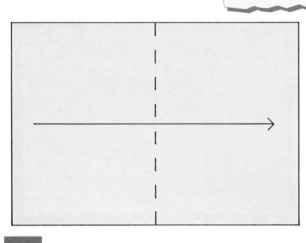

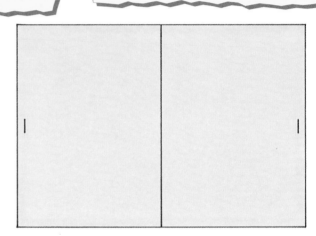

4 Fold the card again, and write your secret message inside.

5 Thread a piece of colored ribbon through both slits and tie a bow.

6 Decorate the front of the card with cut-out pieces of giftwrap, or draw a pattern with markers. You could draw a pattern with a gold pen, and match it up with some gold ribbon to seal the card.

7 For a different kind of secret card, take the card and fold both edges into the center.

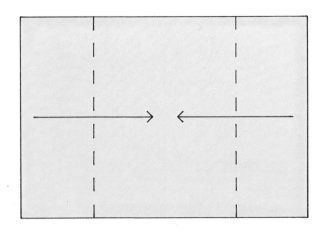

8 Make slits on the two edges that meet in the middle, as you made them before.

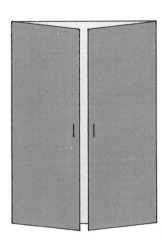

9 Write your message and seal the card with ribbon. Decorate it in any way you like.

WISE OLD OWL CARD

A great, fun card to send to anybody, for any special occasion. Owls are often thought of as being clever and wise creatures—so this card might be just right for a Good Luck card.

You will need
Stiff paper (for the card)
Some colored, stiff paper (for the eyes, feet, and wings)
Scissors, glue, or tape
Three round things to trace around (or a compass)

1 Fold the paper in half the short way. This is the basic card.

2 Cut out six circles, two large (about 3 inches or 8 cm across), two medium, and two small. Use a different color for each size.

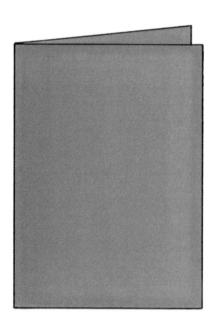

3 Glue the large circles onto the card, at the top as shown. Then glue the medium and then the small ones on top.

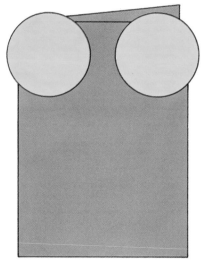

4 To make the claws, cut out a circle from a piece of paper the same size as the largest circle for the eyes. Cut it in half.

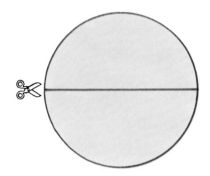

5 Draw equally spaced lines, 1 inch (2 cm) long from the flat side of the semicircle. Cut along each line.

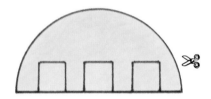

6 Cut out every other piece; stick the claws on to the bottom of the card.

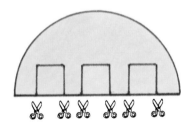

7 For the nose, cut a triangle from the paper. Fold the triangle in half lengthwise. Stick it to the card between the owl's eyes (it is easier to stick this on with tape).

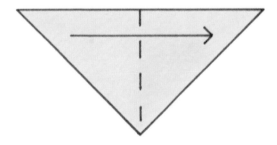

8 Fold the colored paper in half lengthwise, and cut along the fold.

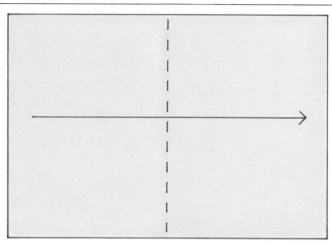

9 Pleat each piece, the short way, by folding about 1/2 inch (1 cm) lengths, first to the front, and then to the back.

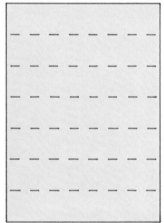

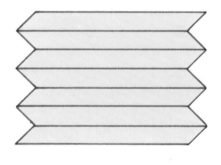

10 Stick these on the sides of the card.

11 Wise Old Owl Card.

GIFT TAGS

Every gift must have a little tag to say who it's for and who it's from. It's great fun to save used greeting cards and recycle them into gift tags.

Patchwork Tags

Stick leftover scraps of colored paper and giftwrap on small blank cards to make the perfect tag for each present. You can match the tags to the giftwrap on your present for a very stylish gift.

You will need
A piece of stiff colored paper about 5 inches by 3 inches (13 centimeters by 8 centimeters)
Scraps of colored paper and patterned giftwrap
Pencil, scissors, ruler
Glue, ribbon

1 Cut several squares, triangles, and strips from the colored paper and giftwrap. They will need to be quite small to fit on your tag.

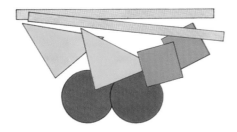

2 Lay the pieces on the card. When you are happy with your pattern, glue the pieces down.

3 Make a hole and thread the ribbon through.

4 You can experiment with all kinds of shapes and patterns.

5 Gift Tags.

CUT-OUT TAGS

Add an extra dimension to your tags. You can make them for all kinds of occasions. Here are just some suggestions.

★ ★

You will need
Stiff colored paper
Small scissors
Felt-tip pens

1 Take a piece of stiff colored paper, 5 by 4 inches (13 by 10 cm) and fold in half lengthwise. Unfold it so it lies flat.

2 With a felt-tip pen, carefully draw a flower on the paper, partly over the fold line.

3 With the point of your small scissors, make a small hole on the part of the picture ABOVE the fold line.

4 Cut along the pen mark, only for the section that is above the fold.

5 Fold the tag along the fold again, and the section you have cut should stand up at the top. Color and decorate your flower any way you like.

6 Cut-out Tags.

Hint

Write the message in your tag after you have cut out the picture, otherwise you may find part of your message is missing!

More suggestions

Make Christmas cards with a cut-out Christmas tree, Easter cards with a cut-out egg. You could even have cut-out boats, space rockets, animals, and birds.

MAKE YOUR OWN PAPER

We use paper every day, but have you ever thought about how it is made? You can find out by following these directions. It's quite easy and great fun. You can produce a sheet of handmade paper every few minutes and each one will be different.

It's a great recycling project because you turn old waste paper into beautiful new sheets which you can use to make special greeting cards.

You only need a few supplies. If you cannot find them around the house, you can find them at your local supermarket or other store.

Most recipes for making paper begin with instructions for constructing a mold, which is a double wooden frame. This can take quite a lot of time. I have invented a new way of making a mold with two disposable aluminum foil baking tins. This means the fun of making paper begins right away.

Read through the complete instructions and assemble all the things you need before you start. It's best to work in the kitchen.

MAKING A MOLD

CAUTION: Ask an adult to help you cut the pans, as the edges may be sharp.

1 Cut out the bottom of both pans like this: Turn the pan upside down. With the point of the scissors poke a hole in the middle. Make four cuts out to the corners, but not all the way to the edge. Now you can cut out the bottom of the pan, but leave 1/2 inch (1 centimeter) all around the edge.

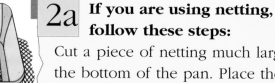

2a **If you are using netting, follow these steps:**

Cut a piece of netting much larger than the bottom of the pan. Place the netting between the two pans and stretch it tightly. Hold it in place by clipping clothespins to the sides of the pans. Because the netting is soft it must be stretched tightly over the sides.

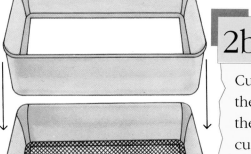

2b **If you are using screening, follow these steps:**

Cut a piece of screening the same size as the bottom of the pan. Place it between the two pans. It must lie flat. If necessary, cut narrow slivers off the edges to make it fit. Clip the sides of the baking tins together with two clothespins. This forms the mold.

MAKING THE PULP

The paper you use every day is formed by mixing wood chips or rags with water into mushy pulp. You can make pulp with almost any kind of paper: used stationery, advertisements, magazines. (Newspapers turn out rather dull, gray paper.)

CAUTION: Do not throw leftover pulp down the sink. It may clog the drain.

You will need
Used paper
A large bowl
A blender

1 Tear paper into small squares into the bowl. Pour in lots of warm water and let the mixture soak overnight. It should be like a very thick soup. If it's too thin, pour off some water. If it's too thick, add some water.

2 Fill the blender about two-thirds full. Blend the mixture for about two minutes.

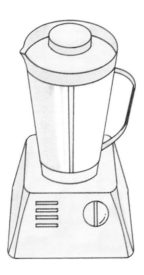

Note: *If you do not have a blender you can blend small amounts of pulp with a hand-held mixer–electric or hand powered. Instead of recycling paper it's best to use tissues because they are soft and will not strain the motor of a hand mixer.*

FORMING A SHEET

1 Cover the bottom of the sink with a layer of water. Put the mold into the sink.
Put some pulp in the measuring cup. Pour the pulp into the mold in a close, wavy line.

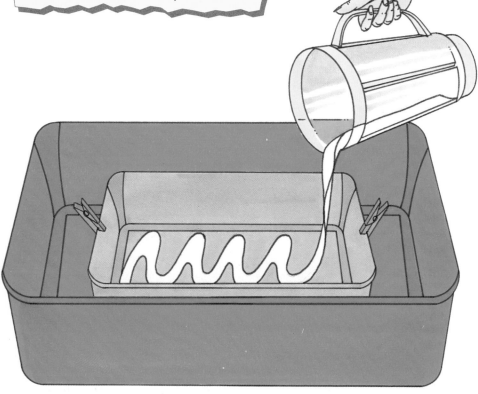

2 Lift up the mold and hold it with both hands. Shake it gently from side to side twice, and back and forth twice. This locks the fibers together into a strong piece of paper.
Hold the mold still for a while and let any leftover water drain into the sink.

DRYING

It takes quite a long time to dry the paper completely. It's easiest to let the sheet dry on the screening (Method 1), but then you have to wait until you can make another piece of paper on the same screen. Instead, you can dry the paper between absorbent cloths (Method 2).

You will need
Kitchen cloths
Old newspapers
Cover the kitchen counter or table with lots of newspapers.

1 Take the clothespins off the mold. Lift up the screen with the pulp and place it between two cloths. Pat the top cloth gently to squeeze out water.

2a **Method 1: Drying the paper on the screening.**

After you have pressed out as much water as possible, set the screen in a warm place to dry.

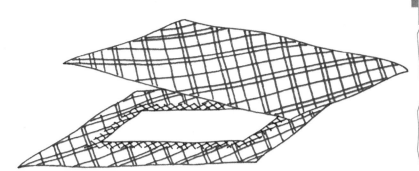

2b **Method 2: Flipping the sheet off the screening.**

Press out as much water as you can between two cloths. Replace them with dry cloths and press out more water. Test one corner of the new sheet of paper to see if it will come away from the screen. If it sticks, press out more water with fresh cloths.

When the corner comes away, you know the paper is ready to be flipped. Place another cloth on top. Flip over the cloth, paper, and screen. Now you can take away the screen.

Add flowers, vegetables, and food coloring

Now that you know how to make a plain sheet of paper, add small pieces of flower petals, broccoli, green leaves, brown leaves, orange juice, and other natural materials. Add them to the pulp a few seconds before the end of the blending.

Decorate greeting cards

The illustrations show some of the ways in which you can use handmade papers on greeting cards.

Paper you can write on

Cover any sheet of paper with spray starch. This is called "sizing the paper." Otherwise the ink may spread in an ugly way.

Rainbow paper

Prepare several small bowls with pulp in different colors. Pour one color after another on the screen in curves like a rainbow. Follow all the other steps to make a piece of paper.

White paper: *blended with dried herbs, wood chips, or flower petals*
Green paper: *blended with geranium petals, with snips of leaves added at the last minute*

Blue paper: *blended with blue food coloring*
Yellow paper: *blended with yellow food coloring*

With your homemade paper you can wrap gifts and create some of the cards and tags in this book.

MORE CARDS AND TAGS

When you have made some of the cards and tags in this book, try experimenting with some of your own designs, colors, and patterns.

Look at this picture; it's packed with all kinds of different paper and materials that you can use to create lovely presents and cards for your friends and family.

If you see any used wrapping paper or ribbon that you like, save it and try to use it for a gift. You can use lots of materials that are usually thrown away. Be imaginative and create something really different!